BLEED AWHILE

AWHILE

Lawrence Scott

DEDICATION

To my father, grandfather, brothers and uncles
who have all shown me in one way or another
how to "fight some more."

ACKNOWLEDGEMENTS

This book is a product of my experiences working with the Army West Point Football team. It would not exist without the opportunities afforded to me by Coach Jeff Monken. Coach Monken, thank you for your leadership, your example, and trusting me to play such an intimate roll with our young men. This would also not exist without the support of my father, Lee Scott Sr. Dad, you will never know how important your support of me leaving home was, especially at time when I may have been needed most. Not many know how much you have sacrificed to stand where you stand. I hope this adds to what you have continued to build as you stand on the shoulders of giants and I stand on yours. Grandpa, the wisdom in these pages are but drips of the overflow I've gained by sitting at your feet. Thank you.

I would also like to thank everyone who's helped create this resource, especially my friend and editor, Dana Tyler. Your dedication, creativity and attention to detail has taken this project to a level I never imagined.

As always, thank you, H.S.

Table of Contents

Before games, head coaches are sure to say something to get their athletes going, but this day was different. The team was nestled tightly in the visiting locker room of the Air Force Academy. The atmosphere tense and anticipation great, the room was in relative silence. The players sat closely situated, listening to their favorite hype songs, visualizing their assignments, saying their last group prayers and performing their various pre-game rituals. Just before the team was to come together and run out onto the field, Coach Monken burst into the locker room enraged. His eyes were ablaze; his face more intense than usual. He pushed past players and coaches to get where people could see him. He began addressing the team. Undoubtedly, with whatever had gotten into him, and with so much time left before it was time to take the field, the team was in for a long, zealous, highly passionate address, right? Not so. In fact, it was one of the shortest pregame speeches he'd given to the Army Football team.

He stood up on a chair and emphatically exclaimed, "I'm going out there to whoop their ass!"

Almost immediately, as if he were looking each player in their soul, he demanded, "Who's with me?" He jumped down and pushed for the door.

Still early, the team was met in the tunnel by a referee and the state troopers that escorted the team. They were motioning coach to hold off to let the Air Force team run out of the tunnel. It did not matter. Coach Monken looked back at the sea of players and coaches behind him and in one large motion, as if commanding troops to march on, he waved everyone forward and started charging toward the Air Force team who had yet to run out. Coach marched the team toward the light blue gaggle of players until the officials and troopers wouldn't allow it any further. Still raging, coach tried to keep going.

The troopers physically held him back! If it weren't for the fact that he wasn't wearing any equipment, it would have seemed he was ready to knock somebody's head off.

Despite the inspiration and hard-fought efforts during the first half, the 2-6 Army team, with no hope of a chance at a bowl game or even a winning season, returned to the locker room down 0-10. The score of the game, however, did not defeat this team. They did not quit; neither did Coach Monken. When it was time to go back out on the field, Coach rallied the players behind a chant that had become the rallying cry of the rest of the season.

"I'm going to fight until I cannot fight anymore.
And when I cannot fight anymore,
I'm going to lie down, bleed awhile, get up,
and fight some more."

For the next half, the team did just that. They fought. The game ended, 3-20, Air Force, but that game proved that something was different. After that display, two things were apparent about this team; they were fighters, and there was no quit in them. The Army team ended the 2015 season 2-10. But the corner had been turned. They had learned to fight. More importantly, they had learned how to get up and fight some more.

Sometimes, life will knock us down. We may have to lie down to bleed awhile. But we must also learn and remember how to heal so we can gather the strength to get up and fight some more. Otherwise, while lying down, we will stay there, never to rise and fight again. This is a situationally responsive playbook. Built to attack and defend; it is both offensive and defensive. In the fight of life, we will all bleed awhile. The fighters will get up to fight some more.

This playbook is dedicated to the fighters.

STRESS

Stress is unavoidable. Whether it is a relationship, an activity, a subject, or even a memory, everyone will deal with stressors. Believe it or not, stress is a good thing. It is an indication that there is something to which we need to pay closer attention. Stress keeps us alive. During stressful events we may experience elevation in heart rate, senses, and even blood pressure. All these physical indicators are present to prepare our body to respond to whatever is triggering us. It should not be our goal to rid ourselves of stress, but we must learn to manage it.

There are many ways to manage stress. One powerful method is to change your perspective about what that stress means. Usually, when we are in stressful situations, we attach that stress to a fear rather than a function. If we change our perspective to functionality, we can prepare ourselves for the next time the stressor is presented. When we encounter stressors, we should look at them as opportunities to work on the areas that stress us out.

If we are presented with a relationship that stresses us out, we should look at that relationship as an opportunity to prepare us to be more effective in relationships. If we are presented with a performance that stresses us out, we should look at that performance as an opportunity to prepare ourselves to be better equipped as a performer. Every stress is an opportunity. Work through those stressful moments so that, as those opportunities are continually presented, you can be more effective, more prepared and better equipped. You will never be truly stress free. Learning to master and manage that stress, is an invaluable skill.

Before you know it, you will be in highly stressful situations and functioning at your very best. Stress is inevitable. Learning to manage it will make you successful in areas that others would rather avoid.

PERCEPTION

Have you ever met somebody with negative perceptions about you? Whether it is based on the color of your skin, the community you grew up in, the sport you play or your religious beliefs, people will have their own perceptions of you. Perceptions are simply assumed knowledge. So, how do you deal with negative perceptions that have been formed before you even had a chance to defend yourself?

1. ASSESS the individual's willingness to learn more about you.

Take some time to investigate their disposition. You need to discern whether they are open to challenging their own perception.

2. If possible, MONITOR your time with the individual.

If the individual is not open to seeing you differently, limit how much they see you. Unfortunately, you could do more damage than good if the only thing this person sees or experiences from you is the defense of that which they are already resolved to believe about you.

If the individual is willing to learn about you and challenge their own perception, offer yourself to them honestly and genuinely. Allow them to see who you are so that their perception can be clarified, whether right or wrong.

How you handle it will have large impact on how you will continue to be perceived. It can also have lasting impacts as your perception can be perpetuated through an individual's sphere of influence.

Remember: if you are dealing with an established negative perception, silence is usually the best defense. It offers no fuel to a fire that inevitably burns out with time.

DOUBT

You will be visited by what you believe. Doubt therefore, must be eliminated. Perhaps one of the most dangerous yet unaddressed inhibitors to recovery and progress is doubt. Subtle uncertainties about accomplishing certain tasks, performances, and accomplishments can settle in the minds of even the most competent individuals. Doubt is a lack of conviction that battles the confidences purposed to take us to the next level. How do you replace this doubt with confidence? How do you replace the uncertainty with a conviction that is impermeable? Rely on what doesn't fail; values.

Values do not fail. In fact, they strengthen confidence because they speak to who you are, not to what you do. When you live, breathe and behave according to your values, it strengthens the character and confidence of self. Backed by your values and belief, there is nothing impossible for you. You must keep your values in front of you. Make them visible. Write them down. Recite them. Memorize them. Whatever you need to do, do it. As you reassure yourself of those infinite and eternal values, your confidence will be built so that there is no task, no performance, no request, nor any environment that you are not strong enough to conquer.

FAILURE

While it is hard to accept, failure is inevitable. It is defined as a lack of success or the omission of an expected action. In other words, failure is falling short of whatever expectation is set. While we may all experience this often, it is important to know that what you experience is not who you are. While you may have fallen short of your own or others' expectations, who you are, is more than that experience.

You are not your failures. On the contrary, your failures are preparation for success. The key to dealing with failure is found in what you are willing to take from it in an effort to prepare you for the next fight. Admittedly, failure can take a lot out of you, but one thing you cannot afford to lose is your fight. You cannot allow failure to take the fighting spirit away from you. No matter how many times you fall, if you do not give up, the lessons you learn coupled with your will to rise again will guide you to success. Regardless of your failures or shortcomings, you must remember who you are!

When failure happens, do not dwell on what you have done, but remind yourself of who you are! Say these things to yourself:

I am resilient!
I am an overcomer!
I am a victor!
I am enough!

Do not let failure discourage your fight. Use it only as a tool of enlightenment to attack your weaknesses and become better every time. Losers let failure become who they are. Winners let failure remind them of where they're going.

PASSION

Passion is a strong, barely controllable emotion. It can be sparked by a reaction to an event or it could be birthed from a deep and sincere connection to people, activities, or things. It is more than affection or care; and different than love. When you are passionate about something, your response to it is innate. It is automatic. And sometimes, before you know it, you can become quite animated. It is like a fire burning inside of you, but no one can carry fire unprotected and not be burned. So, how do we protect ourselves from our own passions?

It is through discipline, planning, and the acquiring of knowledge that we take deliberate steps to slow the automation of our passion. The beautiful thing about planning with sound counsel and good information is that it does not dull your passion. On the contrary, it serves to increase the focus and intensity of that internal fire because it builds the routines, plans and systems that protect us from getting burned out.

If you commit to being disciplined, to planning and to gathering knowledge, you can be equipped to engage your passions without getting burned. It will put checks and balances on your immediate, natural, and passionate behaviors. When you rehearse these practices enough, you will begin to enjoy your passions more as you will see better results and more productivity. It is not always easy, but it is necessary. Unbridled passion is reckless. Protected passion is increasingly productive.

DISTRACTIONS

No matter the time, place, or environment, distractions will always be present. There is always an opportunity to lose focus on the task at hand. Any time you are prevented from giving your full attention to something, you are distracted. Whether it is by music, TV, social media, or someone making funny gestures, if it takes a portion of your attention or cognitive effort, it is a distraction. One reason we are distracted is that we have gone on autopilot.

Sometimes, we have done something for so long or we have done something so many times that we do not actively think about what we are doing. Instead, we think about what we had for lunch that day, or how you were upset because your favorite show was cancelled, or we think about the message we sent to our crush and wonder whether or not they will respond. Sometimes, we even allow our eyes to look at what someone else is doing, rather than being engaged in what we are doing. No matter how many times you have done it or how long you have been doing it, you must keep focused on what you are actively doing. When you lose focus, you can miss vital details or information that can affect your next move.

Another reason we become distracted is that we devalue what is right in front of us. We start comparing how green the neighbor's grass is. What may look or seem more appealing from a distance may not necessarily be all it is cracked up to be. You must be committed to your own process. Stay focused on what you have to do. Keep your mind engaged. As you do that, you will find the appeal of distractions severely decreasing. You are far too important to compare yourself to someone or something else. Your goals are far too important to be distracted by what other people are doing. Before you commit to anyone or anything, commit to yourself. Commit to the growth and personal success that is sure to come from what you and you alone can do. The distractions will still come, but they will not be able to stay.

LET DOWNS

Whether we acknowledge it or not, we all have expectations of our lives and the people in them. And whether we like it or not, those expectations will not always be met. When someone or something falls short of the expectations you have set, you will experience let down. In life, we will all be let down at one point or another. It can happen in many forms.

Maybe you have experienced unfulfilled promises. Maybe someone did not hold up their end of the deal. Maybe you have given more than what was reciprocated. But how do you come back from that? How do you learn to trust again? What do you do when you have been let down?

First, you must learn to hold people accountable. The key to accountability is that it starts from within. The more you hold yourself accountable to your own expectations, the easier it will be to hold others accountable. It also serves as an example to those around you that they will be held accountable to the same degree that you hold yourself accountable. But what about dealing with pain from being let down?

Perhaps the most effective yet challenging strategy, in the moment, is to remember your own shortcomings. The most sobering reflection is to recall the times you have fallen short of others' expectations. If you can remember the areas that you have fallen short, you can loosen your grip on the shortcomings of other people and the expectations of life. Expectations are a good thing but when those expectations are not met, you cannot allow that to keep you from moving forward.

So, how do we deal with let downs? Learn and practice accountability of yourself, first, and accountability of others second. While still holding others accountable, forgive them and let go, remembering your own frailty. Surely, as we have recognized the humanity in ourselves, we must also be willing to recognize and appreciate the humanity of others.

BETRAYAL

Even more hurtful than let down is betrayal. When someone you trust is willing to expose you to danger, disadvantage, or adverse conditions for the sake of personal gain, it is truly hurtful. There are a few people, groups, and entities who hold loyalty in high regard. Even in those groups, there may still be someone willing to betray them all.

The best protection from betrayal of trust is found in where we put our trust and loyalty in the first place. No matter who they are, the people in your life are still human. They are not perfect. You must shift your trust from people to the intangible and eternal values they exhibit. In other words, trust only in what you know will never change or waver.

When you trust values and character rather than the people who exhibit them, it forges a trusting yet critical disposition. You will be able to evaluate, daily, the character of that individual. You will look for the patterns of values in people rather than assume that they are there. This is a challenge. Values are often best evaluated through individuals. It may be difficult to separate the individual from the values or character traits that the individual possesses; however, if you look to and make decisions based on values rather than personalities, heredity, or title, when the fallibility of human nature is revealed, you can save yourself headache and heartache. For, it was never the person in whom you put complete trust, but rather the positive intangible values they have exhibited up until the moment of betrayal.

INADEQUACY

If I told you that you had everything you needed to be successful would you believe me? If I said that every trait, every ability, every skill, every single connection that you needed to make it to the next level or to complete your current purpose is already in your hand, would you believe me? If the answer is no, you may be battling inadequacy.

When you feel you lack a particular quality or the desired quantity of something needed to accomplish a task or purpose, you may consider yourself or your environment inadequate. We all feel inadequate from time to time. We know what we desire next, but what we have or where we are does not seem good enough to get it. One thing to do is master what you have now. If you master what you already have and where you already are, you will find yourself inching closer and closer to where you want to be.

Look within yourself to find the gifts, talents, skills, and connections that you already have. Focus on these things rather than what you do not have. As you do, you will see how what you already have can be used to strengthen yourself to fight some more.

It may not be easy, but it is possible. Believe in yourself. Remind yourself of who you are and what you have. Sometimes, you may not think you have a whole lot. But little is made much when you believe that who and where you are today will take you where you want to be.

SETTING EXPECTATIONS

If you find that you feel let down or betrayed more than you would like, or if you find your effort in situations or relationships is not being reciprocated, it is possible that you are dealing with a mismanagement of expectations. While feeling constantly let down may hurt, there may be a simple fix. You may just need a better way to set and manage your expectations.

Having expectations is not a bad thing. However, we can set ourselves up to feel let down, sad, or dejected if we do not properly communicate and manage expectations. The best way to manage our expectations of others is by doing two things:

Communicating

When you have expectations of a person or group, it is important to explain those expectations directly, clearly and specifically. If you can communicate your expectations honestly, it affords others the opportunity to let you know whether or not they can meet those expectations. People cannot be held responsible for what they have to guess or assume. You must be honest with yourself and others. Otherwise, you will become frustrated with people for not doing something they had no idea you wanted.

Listening

Once you have communicated your expectations, it is important to allow others the opportunity to accept or reject them. You must listen so that people can communicate any issues they may have with meeting your expectations. When listening, you must pay closer attention to what is meant than to what is said. In so many words, someone can and will let you know whether they agree or are willing to meet your expectations. You must be willing to hear the intent. You cannot coerce people into agreement. It must be organic. By constantly communicating and listening, you can continually manage expectations.

INJURY

Hurt does not always happen slowly. Injury does not always happen in an instant. Whether it occurs slowly or swiftly, we are all susceptible to being injured or hurt. If you are physically injured, your body will let you know that something is not right. It will send signals to your brain to let you know that a particular area of your body is in need of extra attention. You may lose functionality. You may lose range of motion. You may experience pain or discomfort. Whatever the signals may be, they are warning signs to let you know that it is time to pull back and heal.

Just as we experience physical injury, we all experience personal injury. We also receive warning signs for these emotional injuries too. We feel when something is not quite right. We will know when something is not working the way that it should work. You will sense it when the corny jokes that always made you laugh are not working anymore. When your energy and motivation to get out of bed in the morning is not the same as it used to be, you may be emotionally or spiritually injured.

When we injure our bodies, we use the acronym R.I.C.E as a remedy: Rest, Ice, Compress, and Elevate. Very similarly, in times of personal, emotional injury, we can follow a similar procedure-- The four Rs; Rest, Release, Relate, and Relax.

We must REST to give ourselves time to recover.
We must RELEASE and allow ourselves the opportunity for peace even while it still hurts.
We must RELATE to others to assure ourselves that we are not alone.
We must RELAX to release the pressure of being better too quickly.

Healing from personal emotional injuries, much like physical injury, is a process. It is okay to not be okay, but you cannot stay that way. Go through the process of healing personal injuries so that you can be complete and more effective with nothing holding you back! Resist the pressure of trying to be healed immediately. Any process that is rushed has the potential to cause more damage than the healing you intended.

MISTREATMENT

It would be naïve to think that everyone we encounter will treat us the way we would like to be treated. It is also naïve to suggest that people will always place us in positions that are in our best interest. Everyone we encounter does not always have our best interests in mind. When we encounter these people, we may experience mistreatment. So, how do we respond?

Most mistreatment has more to do with the one mistreating you than it does you. It is true that hurt people hurt people. It is also true that selfish people cause damage to others because of their lack of consideration. Though it is difficult, when we encounter mistreatment, we must remember and consider where that individual is emotionally. While they may not consider us, it does our heart well to consider them. Through empathy, we can consider their mistreatment a reflection of where they are psychologically or emotionally, rather than take their actions personally.

When you empathize with their experiences or perspectives, it not only allows you to endure a little more, but it also shows others an example of how you would like to be treated. We must deny ourselves the satisfaction of retaliatory impulses. The platinum rule has no amendments or clauses. Treating others, the way they'd like to be treated has no addendum. It applies to everyone; even those who mistreat you. The more you can treat others the way they would like to be treated, regardless of their treatment of you, the more you will receive the treatment you would like to see yourself. It is not an easy task, but a necessary one. Keep fighting.

SET-BACKS

Have you ever been delayed? Have you ever experienced a set back? They can be quite discouraging or even feel crippling. Our displeasure or disappointment is often caused by a hope or expectation that has yet to be met. It comes from various places. However, our disappointment is often premature. Sure, sometimes we are disappointed in people, but what about when we are disappointed with our situation in life?

You see, our plans almost never come together the way we planned it. We encounter roadblocks, delays; we may even encounter loss. But if you can positively affirm that your hope or expectation is just, then you mustn't allow the setbacks or delays to discourage or disappoint you. Your expectations can still be met. Your goals can still be attained. Your hope can still be fulfilled. Just keep going. Do not quit. Do not let disappointment settle in and become a permanent fixture in that area of your life.

While you may not be there yet, or your vision is not yet totally realized, if you know it is a just cause, you owe it to yourself to keep fighting. It will happen when it needs to happen. Just do not quit. If your hope, vision, or dream is an inspired one, it cannot die. Keep grinding. Keep working. Keep Fighting. Your hopes will yet be fulfilled; and your expectations realized.

IDENTITY

One of the hardest questions to answer is who are you? It is a deep one that goes past your name, date of birth, hometown, or favorite food. It digs at the core of your being. It even strikes at the purpose for which you have been put here on earth.

Identity is defined as *the fact of being who or what a person or thing is*. In mathematics, identity is defined as *transformation that leaves an object unchanged*. If you consider these two definitions, it may help you identify who you really are.

In other words, when all else is done, and you have slowed your activity, what remains? When there is no more school, work, or sports, who is left standing there?

You see, what you do is not who you are. Who you are has far more to do with how you do what you do. If you carry every task out with tenacity, what remains is a tenacious person ready for the next challenge. If everything you do you do with love in your heart, what remains is a loving person. Your identity permeates through your being. It is your calling card. When those that know you best talk about who you are, they speak on your identity. When you find that everything you have known comes to an end and you are faced with the question or feeling of not knowing who you are, think on these things. Think about what is left after it all is gone. What remains? What character remains? What values remain? These make up who you are.

Whoever you are, whoever you truly are, be bold and honest enough to be that person all the time. As you live with an unbreakable connection to those values, you will find that your identity will carry-on in anything you do, regardless of the situation. Even when what you do is done, who you are will carry on.

LONELINESS

No one wants to be surrounded by people all day every day. We all enjoy being able to get away from time to time. Nevertheless, when solitude is prolonged it can lead to loneliness.

There's a sadness that comes with loneliness that indicates that suggests that being alone is negative. However, when we find ourselves feeling lonely, there are couple things we can do to change the sadness of negativity into the optimism of opportunity.

The man who relies solely on others for his sense of self-worth and connection will soon find that he does not know who he is. When you find yourself in times and spaces where there is no one around, it is a perfect opportunity to do what many people fail to do; dive into and connect with yourself. Not only is it a time for you to connect with yourself, but it is a time to connect to what you believe. Whether it is your values, your religion, or beliefs, you can connect deeper unimpeded by the noise of the world. There are some things about yourself that you will only learn when thrown in the fire of leadership, or social experiences. But there are far more intimate things that you could never learn about yourself unless you are alone.

Moments of solitude provide inspiration, clarity, and motivation that come from a divine place within you that the noise of others often drown out. The sadness you feel of being alone cannot be trusted. It is a distraction from all the inspiring possibilities that await you in times of silence. Yes, connection and community are vital. However, so are moments of solitude and silence. Those moments are gifts. Open those gifts with excitement, curiosity, and intrigue. You'll be glad you did, as you find the great and hidden things that await you.

PURPOSE

Why are you here? Why do you exist? What is your purpose? The sad reality about these three questions is that they are often left unanswered by people searching to find the solution. We often make "purpose" complicated and elusive when it is not. Everyone has a purpose, but no one can tell you what yours is.

It is built by a collection of experiences and moments of inspiration that hint at why we exist. There are two important things to know when trying to answer the question of your purpose. The first thing you must identify is what you are passionate about. You must know the one thing that causes you to elevate and become excited. You must identify the thing that you can never seem to stop thinking about; the thing that always seems to nag at you until you can do something about it. The second thing to know is your talent or talents. You have to know what you are gifted to do. What do you do with ease that others must use a lot of effort and concentration to do? You must identify your skills.

Your purpose is discovered at the intersection of your passion and your talents. If you are passionate about international trade and incredibly skilled at making films, perhaps your purpose is to create conversation through film about international trade. If you are passionate about sports and extremely talented at teaching, perhaps your intersection is coaching. Whatever it may be, no one can tell you but you. Whatever skills and talents you have, there is a unique way for you and only you to connect to your passion. And when you find that purpose, no one will be able to do what you do, the way you do it, with the passion that you do it.

DEMAND

Have you ever had a moment where it felt like no matter what direction you turned, you had something else to do? Life can move fast and can demand a lot out of you. Sometimes, you can demand a lot out of yourself. Whether you deal with demands at work, school, relationships or all the above, it can be overwhelming. However, as the demands amass so should your strength, confidence and drive to complete them.

Whatever you magnify in your mind will become larger and larger. As the demands flood in, magnify and strengthen your belief that you can do it! You have the strength, skills, patience and planning to do whatever is placed in front of you. Sure, you may have a lot asked of you at one time; however, these opportunities and challenges are not afforded to everyone. You have been given a gift in the form of challenges and opportunities. Attack them with boldness and confidence. Tell yourself that you can and will be successful. This positive thinking, affirmation, and declaration will place your mind and spirit in a position to overcome better than any negativity or pessimism will. Magnify your belief of success. You will find yourself a whole lot closer and a whole lot stronger.

After you have framed your mind for success, strengthen your confidence with preparation. Confidence is strengthened through preparation. Surround yourself with the right tools, resources and people that help position you for success in all your endeavors. Through preparation and a positive mindset, what seemed like a mountain of demands, will slowly decrease in size and magnitude. Simultaneously, you will grow in confidence that you are not only capable of accomplishing these tasks, but you are prepared to do so.

LOSS

Loss, in varying forms, can bring on a host of emotions. If you lose something or someone very important, it can invoke feelings of guilt, shame, embarrassment, regret, grief, and a host of other emotions. Whatever your loss may be, there are two principles to always remember:

Rest Intentionally

We often describe rest as something passive, as if it just happens. But often, when we experience a loss, rather than resting, almost instinctively we become active and try to work ourselves over it. We work as if being busy will help us to get over what we lost, or at best distract us. Just as active and intentionally as we work, so should we rest. When you are not at ease and your heart is grieved, rest is sometimes the hardest thing to do, but it is a necessary step to recovering the energy you need to get up and go on with life. Sooner or later, you will experience and appreciate your own grief. You must fight to get the rest you need to recover.

Avoid All Forms of Strife

When your heart is grieved, it is foolish to engage in conflict. When you have experienced loss, it may be natural to lash out through other means like disagreements, fights or conflicts. Just as you should actively rest, you should actively seek peaceful and quieting situations. These spaces allow you to process and evaluate. You can gain clarity and resolution. Rest coupled with peaceful environments will strengthen your spirit to keep on going and fight some more.

These are not passive or easy courses of action. They are deliberate and intentional responses to loss that help put you in the best position to get up from your loss and fight some more.

LEADERSHIP

Leadership is influence. Whether on a team, in a class, or in an organization, you may find yourself in a leadership role. You can undoubtedly find hundreds of books, articles, and speakers claiming to know the secret to leadership. In some circles, there is plenty debate and even confusion about what makes a good leader. As complicated as it may seem to figure out the mark of a good leader, it is quite simple. There are three things that you should always do:

Do the right thing.
Do your absolute best.
Show people you care.

By doing the right thing and letting integrity be your guiding light, you will never find your influence, motive or honor will not be called into question.

By doing your absolute best, you not only give the people you lead the best you have, as it is what they deserve, but you simultaneously inspire them to do the same.

By showing people you care, you ensure they know that not only is what you do important to you, but they also know that who they are is important to you, as well. Leaders who care for those they lead will always have more people willing to go out of their way to serve the purpose and the person they have chosen to follow.

When you find people lying down, hurt from things not going their way, they may need a leader to step up and encourage them to fight just a little more. By doing the right thing, doing your absolute best, and showing people that you care, you encourage others to do the same. Your example is the best influence you could ever have.

DISSONANCE/DISCORD

Wherever there is more than one person, there is bound to be dissonance or discord. Two people will never always agree on everything. Conflict is inevitable, but it does not have to linger. Any time there is disagreement or lack of harmony with others or even within ourselves, there is only one option: Attack it!

You must attack discord. Discuss, with understanding, whatever the source of the dissonance is. Discussing with understanding does not mean that you must agree, but it does mean that you must agree to attempt to understand one another. In other words, you must be willing to see it through their eyes.

Teams, relationships, and organizations alike will all have their fair share of disagreements and discord. However, you owe it to one another not to speak harshly, but to genuinely seek understanding and resolution. Anytime there is an elephant in the room or tension is allowed to reside unresolved, everyone suffers. You must be willing to deal with it, head on, in order to move forward together. No two people nor any organization can walk together in the same direction unless they agree on the destination.

DISCIPLINE

Any area of your life that you do not control controls you. If we are honest, there are things in our lives that we have a pretty good handle on; and there are other things that we haven't yet put forth the discipline to control.

Discipline is a system of rules or conduct that allow and assist in controlling any given aspect of our lives. It is important to apply the fundamentals of discipline to all areas of our lives because at any given time, one area of our lives can become problematic if left uncontrolled. Even things that start with the best of intentions can become negative if no parameters, rules, or boundaries are put in place.

For example, what starts as a commitment to being bigger and stronger for a competitive sport can turn into an addiction to illegal substances that does more damage than good. What starts off as an intentional effort in a relationship can turn into an unhealthy dependence on a partner. It is important to set and follow boundaries and conditions for every area of your life. If you live by those disciplines, values, rules or strategies, you will strengthen the pursuit of your goals, dreams, and visions without being inhibited by your own personal shortcomings.

PERFORMANCE

You have practiced. You have prepared. You spent hours getting ready for this moment, and now it is time to perform. Performance is the action or process of carrying out or accomplishing an action. It can be stressful, especially when this performance must be carried out in front of onlookers waiting to see whether you succeed or fail. We all have performance moments. Whether in sport, in work, or even in relationships, there are moments when it is simply time to execute. In those moments, it is crucial that we do not become overwhelmed with the fear of failing.

The fear of failure can keep us from enacting the very thing we have prepared for. In those moments, we must hold on confidently, to the confidence of preparation. As you perform, let the assurance in preparation invoke the clarity and confidence you need to carry out the performance without hesitation.

You will not always be successful. You will have some performances that are better than others. But the performances that do not meet your expectations should not be a result of apprehension caused by performance anxiety. Plan, prepare, and execute. Do not fear failure. That fear is futile. It will not help you. It will only slow you down. Let preparation be the space where fear is not allowed. It is the guard that protects the confidence that you will be just fine.

ISOLATION

There are two types of isolation: negative and positive. The negative isolation is often self-prescribed where we, because of life's difficulties or challenges, retreat to our own internal caves with the intention to not emerge until we have "got it all together." It is as if we believe we could fix everything in life on our own, and we retreat to protect ourselves from the perception of needing or wanting any help or community. That is a false sense of strength.

In those moments, it is important to lean on those who are near. It may not always be the person you want it to be, but a neighbor who is close is better than a brother who is far away. We need each other to make it through life. We need others to strengthen our senses, disciplines and talents. When you find yourself in this isolation, you must intentionally and aggressively get out of it through community, communication and honesty.

There, too, is positive isolation. It is not self-prescribed, but par for the course of growth. Sometimes, to grow beyond where are you are, you must go where no one you have known has gone. Even in those experiences, when you find yourself alone in brand new territory, there are new neighbors and new brothers and sisters who are positioned and equipped to help you on that new journey. In other words, sometimes it takes you being by yourself for a while to find the community or family that will help get you to the next level and fight some more. Embrace your journey and embrace your new environments. You will not feel isolated for long.

CONCLUSION

In 1988, British runner, Derek Redmond had finally made it to the pinnacle of athletic competitions--the Olympics. Athletes who have made it to this stage know what it means to push through adversity, as training for such an event is no simple feat. However, before he even had an opportunity to run in the opening heat of the 400-meter race, Derek had to withdraw from the race because of injury. After such discouragement, Derek Redmond was determined to fight and get back to the Olympics. He was able to recover and make his way back to the Olympic stage, but not without difficulty. During those four years, Derek underwent five separate surgeries, including an operation on his Achilles tendon only four months before the Olympic games! One thing was certain after such adversity: Derek was truly a fighter.

In the 1992 Olympics, Derek seemed to have everything lined up for success. He'd had wonderful performances including the fastest time of the first round and winning the quarter finals. He lined up for the 400-meter semi-final and was expecting a smooth and confident race. Judging by his start, smooth and confident seemed to be his lot. However, with about 225 meters left in the race, Derek suffered a torn hamstring. Limping for a few meters and falling to a knee, it was clear that his race was over; and he would not win, nor would he advance to the finals.

Rising to his feet, with both anguish and determination taking their place on his face, what happened next, no one would have expected. While he had been on the ground, Derek made a decision. He decided that, even if he wasn't going to finish first, he was going to finish. Derek got up and kept on going. He didn't run in stride as he had done earlier; he couldn't. He didn't run as fast as he had before; he couldn't. He didn't look comfortable or satisfied, but he kept on going. He hopped, limped and walked his way to the finish line. Derek, having been plagued with injury before, decided that it was not going to take him out of the race again. After fighting to make the 1988 Olympics, withdrawing due to injury, fighting to recover from five surgeries and return to the 1992 Olympics, he was knocked down by injury again, but he got up and fought some more.

When you are making and executing the plans you have for your life, life itself has a say. Unexpected adversity or challenge will most certainly visit you. There may not always be a right or wrong answer. There may not be a clear-cut response or fail-proof formula to fix it. Sometimes, it's as simple as fighting. Deciding in your mind and in your heart that you will finish. Nothing will stop you from finishing. You may not get there when you thought you would, but you will fight and finish. You may not finish the way you thought you would, but you will fight and finish. Your mind must be set. Your heart must be committed. You must be resolved to fight until you cannot fight anymore. And when you can't fight anymore, it's okay to lie down, bleed a while, get up and fight some more.

Equipping yourself to fight some more is what this book is about. Your life is much too important and valuable to stop where you are. In addition to equipping yourself, you should also surround yourself. As Derek Redmond fought to finish his race, he didn't end up fishing alone. With the pain, anguish and clear disappointment on his face intensifying, Derek's father joined him. Waving away those who wanted to stop them, his father, helped him fight his way to the finish line. When you're going through situations in life, it's important to not only be an equipped fighter, but to have equipped fighters around you.

Life is not meant to be spent alone. When our strength is weak, and our confidence is shaken, having others who can help keep you going becomes essential. If there are people in your life that you know care for you and that you can trust with holding you accountable, share this resource with them. Develop a team of fighters who knows that it is okay to lie down and bleed awhile, but who will not let you stay down too long or stay out of the fight.

As you experience various troubles of life, keep these words close. If only as a reminder of who you are, how strong you are, or how to get up and fight some more, keep this book close. Share it with others who may need it and develop your team with it. No matter who you are or what you have been through, you are a fighter. Don't give up! Get up! Fight some more!

ABOUT THE AUTHOR

Lawrence Scott is a West Point graduate and former football player at the Academy. After graduating from West Point, Lawrence, better known as Coach LoSco, served as an officer in the United States Army. He also served as a Young Adults Pastor at Lively Stone Church in St. Louis Missouri. Lawrence is a certified member of the John Maxwell Team, a prestigious Leadership, Coaching, Speaking, and Training Development Program. In 2018, he moved back to West Point, New York to serve his Alma Mater and football team as the Director of Player Development. Lawrence has a passion for developing and training leaders in the areas of personal growth and leadership. It is this passion that led him to write this simple and encouraging guide on how to recover when life knocks us down.

Made in the USA
Middletown, DE
12 December 2021